D1613276

OTHER GIFTBOOKS IN THIS SERIES

Printed simultaneously in 2007 by Helen Exley Giftbooks in Great Britain
and Helen Exley Giftbooks LLC in the USA.

12 11 10 9 8 7 6 5 4 3

Illustrations © Joanna Kidney 2007
Copyright © Helen Exley 2007
Text copyright – see page 94.
The moral right of the author has been asserted.

ISBN 13: 978-1-84634-006-2

Edited by Helen Exley
Pictures by Joanna Kidney

Printed in China

Helen Exley Giftbooks, 16 Chalk Hill, Watford, Herts WD19 4BG, UK.
www.helenexleygiftbooks.com

A HELEN EXLEY GIFTBOOK

Son!

PICTURES BY JOANNA KIDNEY

Thank you
for showing us the world
through undimmed eyes
– as bright and splendid
as we once knew it.

PAM BROWN, B.1928

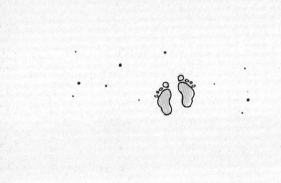

From the very instant
that I saw your big/little feet poking out
from the basket in my room
in the hospital on January 16, 1971,
I have valued and respected
and loved you unconditionally.

ALI MACGRAW, IN A LETTER TO HER SON JOSHUA,
FROM "MOVING PICTURES"

I saw pure love
when my son looked at me,
and I knew that I had
to make a good life
for the two of us....

SUZANNE SOMERS, B.1950

My lovely living boy,
My hope, my hap, my love,
my life, my joy.

GUILLAUME DE SALLUSTE,
SEIGNEUR DU BARTAS, FROM "FOURTH DAY"

Life presents a parent
no greater privilege,
no greater pleasure,
than the opportunity to share
one's son's childhood.

STUART AND LINDA MACFARLANE

It's such a powerful connection;

it takes me by surprise.
I feel like there's a dotted line
connecting me
to my son.

SARAH LANGSTON

With all of the fabulous adventures
I have had in this first half of my life,
it has been our friendship and trust
that have been the biggest gift.

ALI MACGRAW, IN A LETTER TO HER SON JOSHUA,
FROM "MOVING PICTURES"

PARENTS DON'T KNOW
PERFECT HAPPINESS UNTIL
THEY'VE SWUNG THEIR SMALL CHILD
HIGH IN THE AIR
— SHOUTING WITH JOY!

PAM BROWN, B.1928

When nothing's gone right all day
and you're feeling the weight
            of every failure,
      it only needs the rush of small feet

* * *. * * * ** * * ** * * * * * * * * ** * * * *

pounding down the path,
a leap, arms locked around about you,
a grin, a pouring out
of the day's news
– and everything goes your way.

PAM BROWN, B.1928

Dear Son
– I like you, love you, as you are.
But I hold in my heart
all the sons you've been
over the years –
and like and love them all.

PAM BROWN, B.1928

Proud parents boast a little
of their son's abilities
and his achievements.
But glory in his kindness,
his gentleness,
his quiet courage.

PAM BROWN, B.1928

"Which one?"

DWIGHT D. EISENHOWER'S MOTHER,
ON BEING ASKED
IF SHE WAS PROUD OF HER SON

You share his dreams,
his fantasies and his ambitions
and feel a responsibility
to be his guide through life....

LAWRENCE DALLAGLIO, B.1972,
FROM "THE TIMES MAGAZINE", JUNE 18, 2005

A boy's will is the wind's will.
And the thoughts of youth
are long, long thoughts.

HENRY WADSWORTH LONGFELLOW (1807-1882),
FROM "MY LOST YOUTH"

You are a human boy, my young friend.
A human boy.
O glorious to be a human boy!...
O running stream of sparkling joy,
    to be a soaring human boy!

CHARLES DICKENS (1812-1870),
FROM "BLEAK HOUSE"

A SON IS...
the voice who reverses
the telephone charges
from Morocco
and says he knows you
will not mind.
(Which, of course, you don't.)

PAM BROWN, B.1928

As soon as children arrive in your life,
your house and your eardrums
              are no longer your own.
   Your pain is distinctly and singularly
yours, but everything else –
              time? privacy?
                        biscuits?
         Kiss them goodbye.

MARTIN PLIMMER, FROM "KING OF THE CASTLE"

A scabby knee is a thing
of infinite satisfaction to a small boy.

CHARLOTTE GRAY, B.1937

Sons fling themselves.
They bounce, bump,
duck, dive, slide,
pound, paddle, fidget – and fall.
Then they pick themselves up
and do it all again.

PAM BROWN, B.1928

Once Knute playfully demanded
of one of the boys an account of his age.
He answered, "Seven."
"Impossible," his father said,
"no young man could possibly get
quite so dirty in seven years."

BONNIE ROCKNE,
FROM A NOTE IN HER HUSBAND'S
AUTOBIOGRAPHY

SONS EAT ODD SOCKS,
SHOES, BEST SHIRTS,
UNDERPANTS,
ELASTIC AND COMBS.
THERE IS NO OTHER
EXPLANATION.

ROSANNE AMBROSE-BROWN, B.1943

Wife, the Athenians rule the Greeks,
and I rule the Athenians,
    and thou me, and our son thee;
let him then use sparingly
        the authority which makes him,
    foolish as he is,
    the most powerful person in Greece.

THEMISTOCLES
(c.523-c.458 B.C.)

Sons, from the very first, have a totally

different conception of time
to that of their parents.

PAM BROWN, B.1928

Sons always remember where the cakes live.

PAM BROWN, B.1928

He makes fuzz
come out of my bald patch!

CHARLES A. LINDBERGH (1902-1974),
ABOUT HIS SON'S DRIVING

A SON CAN BE
GUARANTEED TO ASTOUND YOU
ALL THROUGH HIS LIFE
— ASTOUND, BEWILDER,
UNNERVE, FLABBERGAST...
YOU NAME IT. HE'LL DO IT.

CHARLOTTE GRAY, B.1937

Sons never seem to listen
and one sighs and dismisses one's advice
as so much wasted breath.
Only to be caught up short one day
by a statement that has
an oddly familiar ring.
He is quoting an impeccable source
to back his argument – you!

PAM BROWN, B.1928

A child enters your home
and makes so much noise
for twenty years
you can hardly stand it
– then departs,
leaving the house
so silent
you think you will go mad.

DR. J. A. HOLMES

...whatever sense of hurt
or injustice a man may hold,
    he knows, in the depths of his soul,
that his mother is waiting always
        for his return.

DAME ENID LYONS (1897-1981)

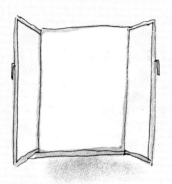

The child may be father of the man,
but if you look closely into
your own son's eyes,
you'll probably see
your father staring back at you.

JON STEWART, FROM
"THE SAN FRANCISCO EXAMINER", JUNE 14, 1986

Long before a mother
    ceases to take care of her son
he has surreptitiously started
                to take care of her.

PAM BROWN, B.1928

A mother is proud of a son
who works hard,
                passes his examinations,
        does well in his job.
        But proudest of all
when she sees him in a happy marriage,
        laughing with his little children,
telling good tales,
                ...loving and beloved.

HELEN THOMSON

The best thing
in a parent's life is to see him,
long after
he has grown and gone,
surrounded by the things he loves,
skilled, useful,
happy
– and yet the lad
they've always known.

PAM BROWN, B.1928

If I have
a monument in this world,
it is my son.
He is a joy, a sheer delight.

MAYA ANGELOU, B.1928

Nothing can come
from your workshop,
however rough and unfinished,
that will not give me
more pleasure
than the most accurate thing
anyone else can write.

SIR THOMAS MORE (1478-1535),
TO HIS SON

I cradled the tiny you,
I nurtured the growing you.
Now I like to admire the big you
– My special son.

HELEN THOMSON

There is something
very reassuring
in a tall son
walking beside you.

PAM BROWN, B.1928

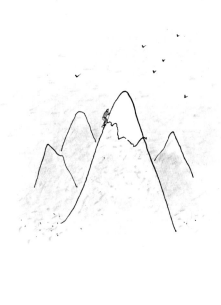

Parents have dreams for their sons
– but the sons have dreams
of their own.
May they all come true!

PAM BROWN, B.1928

A son leaves home
and there's a gap
in one's life
that will never completely close.

HELEN THOMSON

My Son.

My good companion.

My comforter. My helper

and my friend.

CHARLOTTE GRAY, B.1937

Thank you for filling a place

in my life that no one else could.

PAM BROWN, B.1928

May the coming years
bring you new hopes,
new beginnings,
new adventures, new discoveries.

PAM BROWN, B.1928

...the power a child has over you
lasts a lifetime.

BETTE DAVIS (1908-1989),
FROM "THIS 'N THAT"

YOU HAVE MY LOVE AND PRIDE
AND CARE. ALWAYS.

HELEN EXLEY

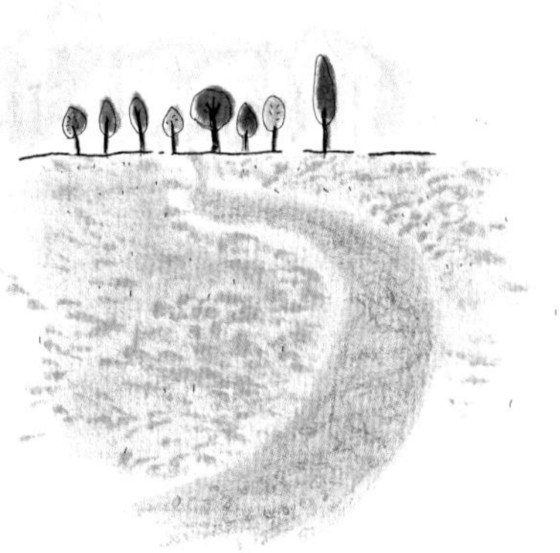

Helen Exley runs her own publishing company which sells giftbooks in more than seventy countries. She had always wanted to do a little book on smiles, and had been collecting the quotations for many years, but always felt that the available illustrations just weren't quite right. Helen fell in love with Joanna Kidney's happy, bright pictures and knew immediately they had the feel she was looking for. She asked Joanna to work on *smile*, and then to go on to contribute the art for four more books: *friend*, *happy day!*, *love* and *hope! dream!* We have now published nine more books in this series, which are selling in 27 languages.

Joanna Kidney lives in County Wicklow in Ireland. She juggles her time between working on various illustration projects, producing her own art for shows and exhibitions and looking after her baby boy. Her whole range of greeting cards, *Joanna's Pearlies* – some of which appear in this book – won the prestigious Henries oscar for 'best fun or graphic range'.